MARS
Colony on the Red Planet

Robyn P. Watts

KNOWLEDGE
BOOKS

Teacher Notes:

Mars is regularly in the news and a new era of space exploration has started. The journey to, and the colonizing of Mars is as important as Cook's Pacific explorations. It offers a whole new world of wonders to explore. It is now technically possible to get to Mars and back. The colonizing of space has been proven with the International Space Station over many years. Now follows the challenge of setting up similar modules on Mars.

Discussion points for consideration:

1. Why was Mars chosen as the next planet to explore and colonize? Discuss the reasons further.

2. Who owns Mars? Should the first country or person to get there own the planet? Compare your discussions with how Antarctica is managed.

3. What challenges will they face? Talk about the importance of problem solving, teamwork, resilience, and goal-setting in regard to this mission. What other attributes would be important?

Difficult words to be introduced and practiced before reading this book:

hydrogen, oxygen, carbon dioxide, satellites, orbiters, colony, binoculars, telescopes, surface, martian, protection, colonized, exposure, radiation, chlorine, twinkle, planet, Mercury, Jupiter, Saturn, Uranus, Neptune, gravity, straight, building, creatures, different, temperature, Fahrenheit, minutes, breathe, difficulties, successful, atmosphere, scientists, equipment, materials, electricity, generators.

Contents

1. Mars - The Red Planet

In the early night sky, you can see a small red dot. Look for this red dot about a third of the way up from the sunset. It does not twinkle like a star, but it looks larger than the stars. If you have a telescope, or binoculars, you can clearly see the planet. This is Mars.

Mars is a planet going around the Sun. It is a lot smaller than Earth. It is about 20% the size of Earth and much lighter. Mars is a long way away - about 155 million miles! It would take about 250 days to get there.

Mars has gases which we cannot breathe. It is loaded with carbon dioxide. This would be poison for people as we need oxygen.

Mars is not the only planet. The other planets are Mercury, Venus, Earth, Jupiter, Saturn, Uranus, Neptune and dwarf planets Pluto, Ceres and Eris.

For a long time, people have made stories, movies and legends about life on Mars. Many people wonder if there is life on Mars.

A long time ago people with telescopes saw straight lines on Mars. They said this was caused by people building canals, or roads on Mars.

Do you think there is life on Mars? Mars has been talked about for a long time. The Mars surface can be seen with telescopes.

We have even given a name to the creatures we think live on Mars; they are called Martians.

Do you think Martians are real?

What do you think a Martian would look like?

7

Mars is a very different planet to Earth, so Martians are not going to look like us. If Martians came to Earth, would they survive on Earth? If humans visited Mars would they be able to live on Mars? Some of the facts we know about Mars show that it is very different to life on Earth. What do humans need to live on Earth?

A human being would die without oxygen and water.

If we went to Mars, we would need to take our own water and food supplies. So, the question remains, do you think Martians live on Mars?

If they did then would they need water to live like us?

Does Mars have water?

Almost all water on Mars today exists as ice. Is Mars able to support life? Or are there Martians who don't need water?

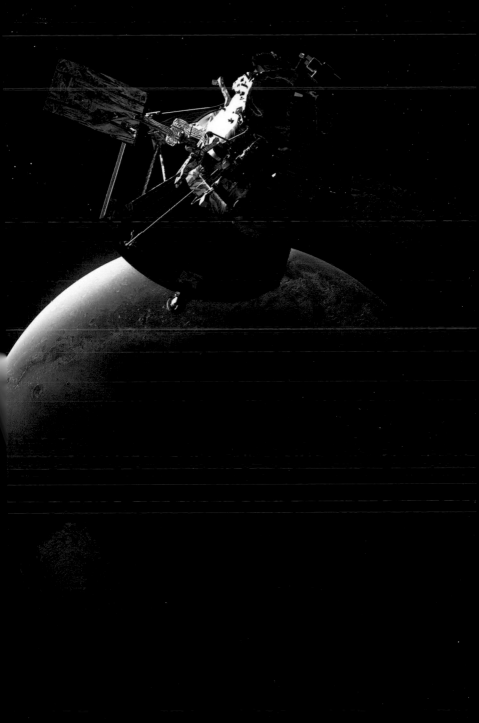

Mars is a colder planet than Earth because it is further from the Sun. The temperature varies according to the season, but is between minus 124 degrees Fahrenheit, and 23 degrees F. This means everything is frozen solid. The Mars climate is like being at the South Pole.

The Martian day is very close in time to Earth's. A solar day on Mars is 24 hours, 39 minutes. Is gravity on Mars like Earth's gravity? No! It is only one third. We know that the Earth's gravity keeps us on the Earth's surface.

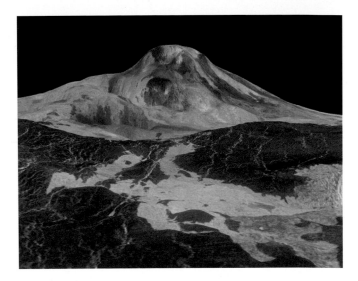

Why go to Mars? What about Venus?
Venus is sometimes closer to Earth
than Mars. It may be quicker to Venus.

Venus would be a furnace. Mars is a
terrible place to live, but Venus would
be ten times worse. The temperature
on Venus is 752 degrees Fahrenheit.
The pressure is like being a mile
under the sea, and Venus has clouds
of acid, not water. Bad idea!

2. Can We Live on Mars?

Plants on Earth provide food for humans to eat. On Earth, plants change carbon dioxide into oxygen. Humans need oxygen to breathe and survive.

Plants on Earth need good soil to grow. On Mars the soil is toxic. The soil on Mars is toxic because of the high levels of chlorine. Plants on Earth cannot grow when the soil contains high amounts of chlorine.

There are many difficulties with humans living on Mars. Humans would need special spacesuits to block dangerous radiation. There is low gravity. The soil is toxic so humans can't grow plants on Mars.

There is a lack of water on Mars. If humans colonized Mars, we would need our own water. The cold temperatures on Mars would make it very hard for humans to survive. Outside of the space cabin it would be freezing.

People are still very interested in exploring Mars. People have not yet landed on Mars. However, since 1965 we have collected Mars data using spaceships. The spaceships use robots to collect data from Mars. This data was sent back to Earth. The countries that have had successful missions in sending unmanned space robots are United States of America, Russia, and India.

3. Exploring Mars

In 1965, the space vehicle Mariner 4 first explored Mars when it passed about 6000 miles above the surface. It took the first close-up photos of the planet's surface. In 1969, Mariners 6 and 7 passed within about 2500 miles of the planet and sent back information about the planet's surface and atmosphere.

In November 3, 1971, Mariner 9 was launched. It reached a Mars orbit, becoming the first US spacecraft to orbit a planet other than Earth.

On December 2, 1971, the USSR's Mars 3 lander made the first successful landing on Mars. It sent data for 20 seconds before failing. In July and August, 1973, the USSR successfully launched Mars 4, 5, 6, and 7. Each spacecraft took about seven months to reach the planet's orbit. Only Mars 6 landed.

In 1975, the USA launched Viking 1. It reached the Mars surface in July, 1976. This was the USA's first successful landing on the Mars surface.

There were many Mars landers used to explore Mars and send back data. The new rovers are doing a lot more work and can be controlled from Earth.

Many countries are talking about a manned mission to Mars. NASA has a plan to get a colony on Mars. This is in three stages of getting to and back from Mars. The total round trip will be over 500 days. This is a long trip.

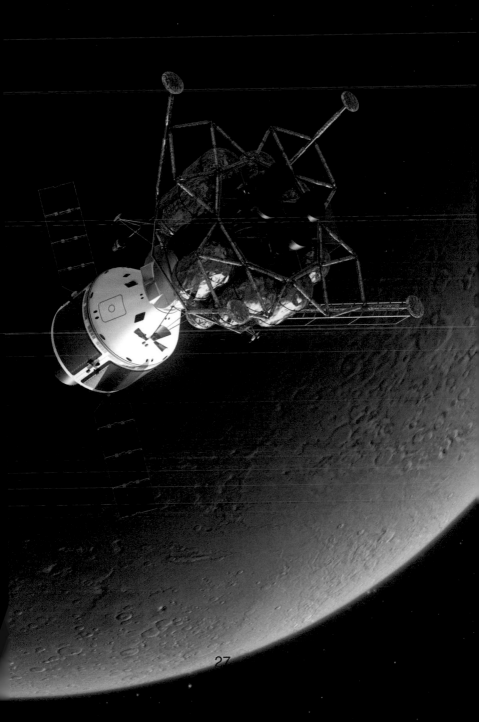

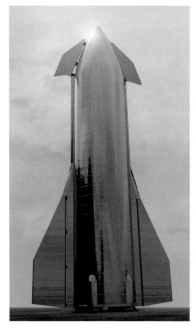

4. Manned Mission to Mars

There are plans to have a colony on Mars. This plan is to firstly get cargo to Mars. The cargo and fuel can use rockets to push the Mars Space Station into a lunar orbit, and then with more power it will be pushed into deep space heading towards Mars. Once it gets to Mars it will start to orbit. Other unmanned cargo craft will follow.

Rockets without people will be sent to Mars. These rockets will land on Mars. They will use drone type rovers to travel over the land.

Their job will be to find water, and make sure the tech is working. They will need working power and oxygen. The cargo ships will bring equipment and supplies. They will get a fuel production plant made and build the base for the colony.

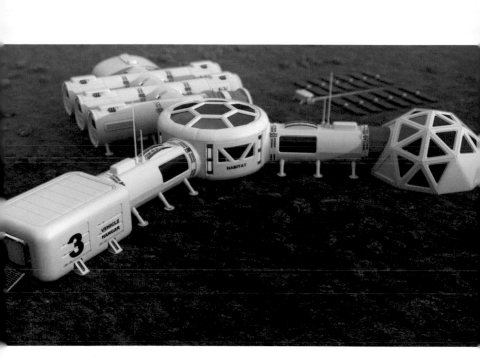

The first thing to do will be to explore Mars. There may be rare metals and minerals in large amounts. Mars will take a lot of effort to explore.

Mars explorer buggies will be needed to go from place to place. Mars has giant winds and storms. The buildings will need special protection from these giant windstorms. These storms blow dust for weeks and weeks. It will not be an easy place to live. Great care will be needed to build the space colony to make sure people can live safely.

5. Mars Colony

Building the Mars colony is going to be a big job. These are some of the things the Mars colony will need:

Water - where will it get the water? There is ice on Mars. It has been seen from Mars probes and satellites.

The surface of the planet shows giant gullies. These have been washed by massive water storms. These storms were a long time ago. The water has gone somewhere. Scientists think it is frozen in great sheets under the surface of red dust.

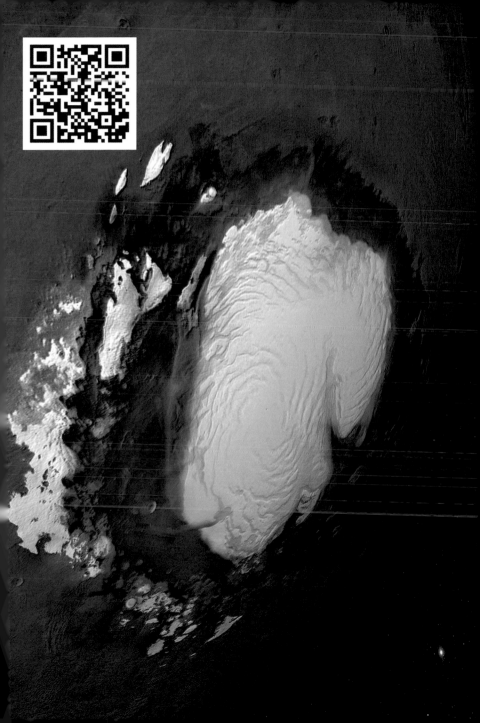

Radiation – the Earth has a protective layer around it which stops the Sun's radiation. Mars does not have any protection from the Sun. The people would need a protective layer or a spacesuit. A helmet would need a sunglass guard to stop the radiation.

Equipment will need protection too. The radiation will break plastics and materials. All equipment will need special metals.

Oxygen – if you smash a water particle you get oxygen and hydrogen gases. Oxygen is needed for our life. We need oxygen to live. We breathe oxygen and give off carbon dioxide.

Oxygen will be used with carbon dioxide from the Mars air to grow plants. The carbon dioxide will be used by plants to make food.

Hydrogen – this is a very important gas. It is a high energy fuel. This could be used to quickly make electricity. It could be used in rockets as fuel.

If you need a buggy, you could take it out through the space hatch and go across the surface. It would be very important to know the Mars weather. This would tell you if a storm is coming. This data comes from the satellite going in an orbit around Mars.

Food – it is possible to grow food on Mars. The food must be grown in special greenhouses. Sometimes dust storms block the sunlight. Food can be grown under blue lamps which help plants grow.

Atomic power systems - may be used to make electricity.

Electricity will be made from small atomic power generators. Solar collectors will help make electricity.

The electricity will be used to make hydrogen and oxygen.

6. Living on Mars

Mars offers a special place in space travel. It is easier to leave the surface. The gravity is not as strong as Earth's. This means it does not need huge rocket engines to get back into space.

Mars could be used to explore the rest of the planets in our solar system.

These are very exciting times. The first thing to do is make a colony on Mars. This is where people will live. They will grow food, collect energy and do science work. Let's occupy Mars!

Word Bank

electricity

hydrogen

oxygen

carbon dioxide

satellites

orbiters

colony

binoculars

telescopes

difficulties

Martian

protection

colonised

exposure

radiation

chlorine

twinkle

planet

Mercury

Jupiter

Saturn

Uranus

Neptune

gravity

straight

building

creatures

different

temperature

Fahrenheit

minutes

breathe